C000135665

STARTING A BATH BOMB BUSINESS

TURN YOUR FUN HOBBY INTO INCOME

SUZANNE CARPENTER

Table of Contents

INTRODUCTION

In 2012, two young sisters from Minnesota started a bath bomb business. They made the bath bombs with different scents, and sold them at craft fairs. Then, they expanded to sell through salons. Over time, they saw so much continued success that by the time they were 14 and 15, respectively, they had a 50,000+ square foot warehouse and a deal with the huge retailer, Target, to sell their bath bombs.

If two teenagers can build a major business selling bath bombs, a business that began with them making the products in their basement, don't you think you could earn some extra income doing the same? Or maybe build a large business just like them?

If you enjoy working with various scents and making bath bombs, then I want to tell you about something that could very quickly begin making you a profitable side income, or better: Making and selling bath bombs. This may seem strange to some, but for others this can be quite simple. If you're already making and selling products from home, then adding bath bombs isn't that difficult. Even if you are starting from scratch it's quite simple to start making and selling bath bombs from home. Let's take a look at how to make bath bombs, how to start a business selling them and how to market so you can actually make a profit.

WHY BATH BOMBS

Before we get into the hows of starting a bath bomb business, let's take a look at the benefits and the reasons why you might want to consider starting a bath bomb business. Simply put, making bath bombs can be done in your kitchen, basement, or garage with just a few simple ingredients and supplies. But there are also several other reasons to consider making bath bombs as your home business.

From a business standpoint the overhead cost of a bath bomb business is relatively low. If you already have most of the ingredients in your home than you may also find you have little to no startup costs as well.

From a product standpoint, bath bombs are fairly simple to make as you'll see in a moment. Bath bombs are also a small and compact item so you won't have trouble finding a place to keep your additional inventory until it sells. The time to product a bath bomb is very short, compared to other potential activities like trying to get traffic to a website.

From a marketing standpoint, bath bombs are something that can be easily marketed and sold both online and offline. Bath bombs are also very easy to customize so you can satisfy a range of customer needs and help to increase your sales. When I teach you how to make bath bombs I'll also show you how you can create some unique fragrance options.

The bath bomb industry is a hot market within beauty and personal care products. Interest in bath bombs has steadily increased in the last five years. People not only shop for bath bombs for themselves, but also as gifts for others. Bath bombs in particular make an excellent holiday gift.

Celebrities have gotten into the mix, too. John Mayer wrote a song about bath bombs. Gwyneth Paltrow has endorsed a line of them. According to Fast Company magazine, interest in bath bomb-types of posts increased at more than 500% in a recent year. The buzz around bath bombs does not seem to be going away anytime soon, and that means good things for you as a purveyor and maker of them.

Lastly, the related niches of aromatherapy and cosmetics are growing at a very strong rate. By making and marketing bath bombs, you will not simply be fighting for a piece of a flat market. You will be selling in to a growing market, one with plenty of demand for new producers like you. Lush, a larger maker of bath bombs with retail stores around the country, is growing at a 25% a year clip, and that is hard to do for a large company. As a small, independent shop, you can probably grow signficantly faster.

Now that we know why you should be making bath bombs, let's see how you can make them and how you can create unique and sale worthy bath bombs.

HOW TO MAKE BATH BOMBS

TYPES OF BATH BOMBS

Knowing that bath bombs is viable niche, and one that is showing promise of giving you a profit if you manage your business well, let's start looking at how you can make bath bombs and start a business from home. The first thing I want to talk to you about is the types of bath bombs you can make. Of course, you aren't just limited to these four types of bath bombs; but it will help you get started with some ideas of what you can create and sell as a part of your business.

The Basic

Even if you aren't familiar with a lot of the cosmetics industry, you likely know what a basic bath bomb is or have at least seen one. They are usually spherical in shape and are available in a wide range of scents and colors. When they are dropped in the bath they will fizz and create bubbles. The basic bath bomb can be infused with a range of essential oils to help create a relaxing bath or other mood enhancing benefits.

Jeweled Bombs

These types of bath bombs are the best option when you want to add a little extra to your bath in the form of something sparkly. There are even a few lines of bath bombs that put jewelry in their bath bombs. This is probably a little beyond your means as a home based business, but it gives you an idea of the possibilities for what you can add to a bath bomb. These types of bath bombs are often purchased as gifts for others.

Glitter Bombs

These bath bombs are best for those who want to have a relaxing bath with a glittery feeling as well. Adding something like glitter, confetti or other sparkly material can make bath bombs a luxury. These beautiful bath bombs are sure to grab the eye of your customers.

Shaped Bath Bombs

This is for when you want to advance beyond the standard bath bomb and really start thinking and workout outside the box. Think of how many unusual and interesting shapes you can make to entice your customers. You even have the option of taking custom orders from customers to really expand your business into offer themed bath bombs for a variety of occasions such as baby showers or business openings. As you can see the possibilities are endless. Let's now take a look at how you can provide variety in your bath bombs with fragrance.

DIFFERENT FRAGRANCES FOR BATH BOMBS

It is really all about the fragrance when it comes to anything related to aromatherapy. Fragrances are one of the key aspects and differentiators of various bath bombs. If you are someone who is particularly good with identifying pleasing fragrances, and someone who enjoys the intricacies of aromatherapy, you may well have a leg up on the competition when it comes to making that bath bomb that everyone will want.

Bath bombs are dropped in water and start to fizz, but people enjoy them for their aromatic properties. Depending on the scent it can influence the mood of your bath time; it can be cleansing, relaxing or stimulating depending on the scent of the bath bomb you choose to use to create your bubbles and atmosphere. While the visual appeal of bath bombs will help your sales, you also want to pay attention to fragrance and the benefits it offers when using it in the bath. There are many types of bath bombs and a variety of scents so you can easily be creative while also taking bath time to a new level. Before you start making your own bath bombs take the time to learn about the ingredients and combinations that help you create a unique variety of scents for your bath bombs.

The Basics

There are plenty of ways to have a refreshing scented bath bomb, but you also want to determine taste, preference and how long a scent should last. To get started designing fragrances for you bath bombs you want to start with noting what shape, color and scent you want for a bath bomb. From there you can come up with your list of ingredients so you have an easy and standard recipe to follow when making your bath bomb.

The scents you choose depend on your ability to mix and match various ingredients, so I'm not going to give you specific recipes. In fact, your ability to create that scent that everyone loves could be what makes you a success story in the bath bomb business. What I will do is provide you a list of the most popular fragrances for bath bombs and what they are known for. Then you can feel free to come up with any unique combination you want to.

Scent Ingredients

Most aroma choices for bath bombs come from botanical sources. You can also choose to add essential oils for therapeutic bath bombs. You can add a range of mixed scents to achieve different goals. The following are some of the most common scents that are easily available, but you are sure to find plenty of other options in your creation of unique bath bombs.

Chamomile is known as a detox ingredients. It offers a deep clean scent that is slightly sweet. However, the sweet notes are what requires it to be used in low concentrations. Chamomile leaves a calming and slightly sedative effect. While it works well with all skin types it is best used for those with damaged or sensitive skin. Since it is a gentle oil it can also be used for children and newborns. The best combinations for this are other floral and citrus scents.

Lavender is a popular scent for bath bombs. The fresh floral scent of lavender provides for a very relaxing bath experience. All skin types will tolerate lavender, even damaged skin. Lavender goes best with rose, wood and needle oils as well as rosemary.

Vanilla is sweet in nature, but offers a very deep scent with calming effects. Although for some, vanilla can also be an uplifting scent. Most vanilla oils are more expensive, but since it is an intense scent a little bit will go a long way. Vanilla works well for all skin types and is best blended with citrus and floral scents.

Rosemary is a wonderful herbal fragrance that has great uplifting properties. It works well for all skin types, but works especially well with oily skin. Rosemary blends best with needle, wood and herbal oils.

Petitgrain is a fresh floral scent with citrus notes. It has the ability to be both uplifting as well as calming. This scent stands out from other citrus scents by being leafier and it has less irritation than other citrus scents. It is best combined with needle and citrus oils.

Lemon is a very sustainable scent that is both sharp and tangy with uplifting properties. It works best with acneic, congested and oily skins. It requires very low concentrations to be an effective scent and it doesn't have any harmful effects. Lemon goes well with nearly all other scents, but doesn't best with rosemary and wood.

Peppermint is a very refreshing fragrance that offers both a cooling and yet stimulating effect. It is great for all skin types and does wonders for opening the sinuses and congested skin types. Peppermint goes with most scents, but does best with needle and herbal scents.

Ylang is an exotic scent that provides a sweet floral fragrance that is slightly tangy. It has aphrodisiac effects and helps to calm. It works well for all skin types and blends well with citrus, floral and wood scents.

Ravintsara is a type of camphor fragrance that helps work as a decongestant. It works great for dry skin and also as a bath addition that helps with sore and stiff muscles or joints. It blends well with citrus, floral and needle scents.

Grapefruit is a citrus scent that is more sweet than others and helps provide an uplifting scent. It works for all skin types, but is best for congested and oily skin. It is a gentle scent, but can be mixed with other oils to help prevent irritation.

MAKING BATH BOMBS

Now that you know about the types of bath bombs that you can make, let's look at how you can make a simple bath bomb so you can get on your way to starting your business inventory. Let's start by making sure you have all the supplies and ingredients you need.

Supplies and Ingredients

Bath bombs are a very simple product to make and only need some basic items. You may even find you have all the basic ingredients you need right in your own home. While you may need a few additional ingredients when customizing your bath bombs. Otherwise the basic ingredients you need are the following:

- Witch Hazel

- Corn Starch

- Mineral Salt

- Desired Essential Oils for Scent

- Citric Acid

- Baking Soda

- Desired Food Coloring for Color

- Light Vegetable Oil

In addition to these ingredients, you'll need the following supplies:

- Two mixing bowls

- Desired molds if you want to make shaped bath bombs
- Whisk

Even if you don't have everything you need already in your home, you can easily get what you need from your local craft store or grocery store. When it comes to the desired molds for your bath bombs you can choose to stick with the traditional sphere shape or you can use a variety of shapes and sizes for molds. For a business, making bath bombs in a variety of shapes, sizes and designs can offer you more variety in your inventory to help increase your sales. Often the best molds to use are the silicone molds that are used for baking or freezing ice. A silicone mold holds up well during the process of making bath bombs plus they are easy to clean and offer a cheap mold option. Just be careful since bath bombs are sometimes crumbly and don't do well in molds with intricate designs or small pieces since they break off easier.

The Process

Once you have all your supplies and ingredients ready, you can start the process of making your bath bombs. Basically it is a simple process of mixing together the wet and dry ingredients in two separate bowls and then slowly combining them into a single bowl.

After combining the ingredients you then just need to pack the mix into your desired mold and place it in the freezer for an hour. The molds need to be very tightly packed and completely filled since you want the bath bombs to be dense in order to come out right. Once the bath bombs are done freezing you can simply remove them from the mold and you are ready to sell your first batch of bath bombs. It really is that simple.

If you aren't selling the bath bombs right away then you can store them in an airtight container. Just remember that the fresher a bath bomb is the more it will fizz and bubble when dropped in a bath. Therefore, you need to take great care when storing your bath bombs to keep them as fresh as possible so your business will be known for the highest quality bath bombs.

The standard ratio for bath bombs is 2 parts baking soda to 1 part citric acid. After you combined the dry ingredients, you can introduce a small amount of liquid to form a wet sand type of texture that is easily moldable. The liquid used is often witch hazel, but you can use plain water or a mixture of oils and butters for additional skin benefits and/or moisture. You can also customize your bath bombs with a variety of fragrance and colors as desired.

Colorants

The coloring for bath bombs is the same concentrated dyes used for food: FD&C and D&C dyes. It is important to use glycerin based dyes so it doesn't cause the mixture of dry ingredients to start fizzing. If you are opposed to using dyes in your bath bombs you can also use micas, clay or other natural colorants. If this is the case then you can add the dry colorants to the dry ingredient mixture. Just remember that dry and powdered colorants will often leave color on the bathroom fixtures as well as your skin.

When adding colorants you can add as much as you want. However, it is best to start with a small amount and add more until achieving the color you want. It is always easier to add more than to remove coloring that is too deep. It is important to note that since baking soda and citric acid are both white in color it is difficult to get bath bombs to be a darker shade such as navy blue or red. If you want a dark colored bath bomb you'll need to use a lot of colorant and this can cause dark bath water or leave a lot of staining behind on bath fixtures and/or skin.

Fragrance

When it comes to adding the right amount of fragrance, there are several ways you can go about it. There are plenty of websites that offer you calculators based on weight or volume so you can determine how much fragrance to add. If this seems like too much work, just do what I do. I simply add a one to two drops of my essential oils, mix and then sniff to see if the smell is appropriate. If you find the scent isn't strong enough you can add a few more drops until you get the desired scent.

Oils and Butters

Choosing whether or not you want to add oils or butters is your decision. Adding these can help improve the skin benefits of your bath bombs. If you choose to add oils and butters to your bath bombs you should add the after the dry ingredients are mixed and smoothed. Any solid butters should be melted down before adding them to the mixture. You also need to be careful with how much you add since too much butters and oils can cause bath bombs to stay soft.

If you are new to making bath bombs, it is best to start with about ½ ounce of oil per 1 and ½ cups of dry mixture. It is also important to note that adding oils and butters to bath bombs can leave behind a slippery residue to the tub and you may want to include a disclaimer with your products to avoid injuries.

Bath Bomb Molds

Perhaps the most important part of making bath bombs is having the appropriate mold. The mold is what brings the bath bomb to life and is the essence of your design. You can use bath bomb molds that are made specifically for the purpose from metal, silicone or plastic; but you can also choose several alternatives as well.

When you are starting a new business one of the deciding factors in choosing a bath bomb mold is likely going to be price. Silicone molds are a great option since they are durable, cheap and come in a larger range of shapes than metal and plastic options. Metal molds, while more expensive, are the most durable and will almost never crack or break. Plastic molds are the most likely to break, but are also the cheapest. Another option for those starting out is to use some common household items as bath bomb molds such as the following:

Ice cube trays work great for molding bath bombs. It also allows you to mold multiple bath bombs at once.

Cookie cutters are a great option since they come in a variety of shapes and sizes.

Measuring spoons are a great option for smaller bath bombs.

Muffin tins work well for creating larger batches of bath bombs. They are also available in both metal and silicone options.

Milk caps and beverage caps can work well for small bath bombs.

With so many options for bath bomb molds, how can you make sure you are choosing the right one? The mold you choose to use can make a big difference in the outcome of your bath bombs so you need to make sure you are choosing the right one. Let's consider some guidelines to help you choose the right bath bomb mold.

First, remember that simpler is often better for bath bombs. There are plenty of shapes and sizes to match the recipe you have. Just remember that the more detailed and complex your design that greater the chance your bath bomb isn't going to come out of the mold right or in one piece.

Second, when it comes to bath bombs; bigger is often better. Bath bombs that are too small often lose their appeal, but too big and they don't hold their shape as well. Therefore, a moderate sized mold is often best.

Lastly, you want to keep in mind the design. A bath bomb mold should ideally have two parts or two halves. This is important because it is easier for bath bomb molding and provides a more professional appearance to your finished product.

Once you have selected your appropriate mold and packed it with your bath bomb material you can move on to the next step.

Freezing

It is best to leave bath bombs in your mold in the freezer for at least several hours. Sometimes you may need to leave them overnight if they are a thicker shape. If you try to remove bath bombs from the mold while they are still soft they are likely to crumble. Make sure the bath bombs are completely dry before removing them from the mold.

Storing

Even with proper storage it is generally a good idea to avoid using bath bombs that have been stored for six months or longer. The longer a bath bomb is stored the more likely it is that it will be exposed to moisture in the air and this can cause a loss of fizzing power. Baking soda and citric acid themselves have long shelf lives, but citric acid will lose its potency the longer it is exposed to the air. Therefore, it is best to make sure your inventory stock is rotated and not sold after being stored for six months or more.

So what do you do if something goes wrong as you're experimenting with your first bath bomb batches? Let's look at how you can troubleshoot your bath bombs.

TROUBLESHOOTING BATH BOMBS

Bath bombs are definitely one of the easier products to make and sell from home. However, as with any craft project it still takes practice to make perfect. Despite the easy process of making bath bombs they are sensitive and can be a little tricky to work with. Bath bombs can potentially crumble, fall apart or fizz wrong. Let's look at some of the common problems you may encounter with bath bombs and how you can correct them.

Cracking or Crumbling

A bath bomb they cracks or crumbles may have too much dry ingredients in the mixture. You can add more witch hazel, oils or butter to increase the moist texture of the mixture. If the cracking or crumbling occurs after removing from the mold then the mixture may be too wet and it is expanding at it freezes in the mold.

Soft Bath Bombs

A soft bath bomb likely means the mixture has too much moisture. Too much witch hazels, oils or butters in the mixing process can be corrected by adding more dry ingredients to balance out the texture. If you are making bath bombs in a humid or wet climate it can also prevent the bath bomb from hardening due to the moisture in the air. You can help the bath bomb to harden by adding a little bit of clay or cornstarch. These can also be added to help make your end product sturdier.

Bumps, Lumps or Warts

A bumpy texture to your bath bomb surface is often the result of clumps in the dry ingredients or not completely mixing in the fragrance oil. Baking soda is particularly prone to clumping together. Before you add other ingredients, it is important to break up large clumps with your hands. For smaller clumps you can choose to pour the dry ingredients through a fine mesh sifter. Doing this can help give your bath bombs a smoother texture.

Warts can also occur on the surface of bath bombs if the fizz contains too much moisture. This is often due to too fragrance or other essential oils not getting mixed enough. Avoid this by making sure the wet ingredients are fully mixed into the dry ingredients.

Lack of Fizz

If you test your batch and find it isn't fizzing as much as you expected then you may want to increase the amount of citric acid in your next batch. Start with 2 parts baking soda in 1.5 parts citric acid and increasing from there. If you are adding cornstarch you can also try reducing the amount of cornstarch used or getting rid of it entirely.

Fizzing can also be reduced if you have too much oils in your bath bombs. As well as fizzing can be reduced when the bath bomb comes in contact with moisture from the air or other damp environment. Consider wrapping your finished bath bombs tightly in plastic wrap to preserve them until the customer uses them.

Expanding Outside the Mold

A bath bomb that expands out of the mold while freezing likely has a mixture that is too wet, meaning the fizzing is occurring prematurely. This often happens if you add a colorant or fragrance oil that contains water. These bath bombs will still fizz when put in the bath, but it will likely be reduced. Bath bombs may also fizz early if they are exposed to moisture in the air. To avoid this try not to make bath bombs on a moist or rainy day.

Not Molding in a Stainless Steel Mold

Sometimes working with a sphere mold can be a little tricky in getting the two halves to stay together. Rather you may notice the bath bomb is sticking to the mold. You can choose to add about 5-10 drops of cyclomethicone to both sides of the mold and swirl it. Allow the molds to drain on a paper towel before inserting the bath bombs to make it easier to remove from the mold. It is also important to monitor the texture of your bath bombs when working with stainless steel molds. The mixture needs to be a little bit on the wet side to allow the mixture to hold shape in a stainless steel mold.

Now that we are set with making bath bombs, let get into how you can start a business selling them.

STARTING YOUR BATH BOMB BUSINESS

So now you know the popularity of bath bombs, what you can make and how to make them. Let's not take a look at how you can start your own bath bomb business and sell these wonderful little personal care items from home. There are several steps involved in starting your business.

CREATE AND TEST YOUR PRODUCT

You can't start a business if you don't have a successful inventory, and one that you know works as intended.

Focus on producing a quality product, and putting mechanisms in to be sure that the quality is there, every single time, in every product. You don't want to start a business and simply start taking orders if you aren't really well prepared to make bath bombs. But it is just as important that you don't simply make a batch and start to sell it without checking to see quality first. Make a few batches and test them yourself or with family and friends first. Make notes on what you discover.

In addition to ensuring the batch is safe, take notes on how they work. How long does the scent last? Does it provide a relaxing and enjoyable bath experience? Does the scent change over time? How does the bath bomb make the water look and feel? Is there anything left that it needs or is there something that needs to be taken away for a better experience? Knowing what potential customers are going to think and feel is important and by keeping thorough notes you'll be prepared for what works and what doesn't.

Finally, as you find a formula and a process that produces a high-quality, consistent bath bomb each time, document specific and exacting instructions. This will be important in the event you ever ask someone to help you make bath bombs, and can be useful as you begin to have many different products. You will be surprised how quickly an important detail could be overlooked.

MAKE EVERYTHING LEGAL, AND COMPLIANT WITH REGULATIONS

This book is intended to help you create a business that complies with all laws and regulations. As with any home business endeavor it is important that you take all the necessary legal steps to be sure your business is operating with full compliance and transparency for your specific product and jurisdiction.

You might need a business license to sell and some cities or states may require additional licenses when selling personal care items. This varies from city to city and state to state, so look into your specific laws.

While not required, you may want to setup your busienss as a Limited Liability Corporation (LLC). It is easier than it sounds, and can help create separation between your personal affairs and business affairs in the eyes of the law. Again, you do not have to setup an LLC, but it is worth exploring.

Make sure you keep good records of your expenses and sales from an accounting standpoint. I always recommend running the business from a new, separate simple bank checking account, not your personal one. This will make it much easier to see what the inflow and outflow is relating to your busienss. Intermingling your personal and business transactions will make financial reporting and year-end taxes much more complicated.

As you begin showing revenue and profit, you will need to file taxes. Don't view this as a burden - paying taxes means you are making money with your business! Research all of the tax rules for your city, state, and country, and know that tax laws change often. Consult a professional if ever in doubt.

You'll also need to know that, as of this writing, bath bombs are regulated as cosmetics by the FDA. That regulation involves specific rules on acceptable ingredients, labeling, and other guidelines to follow. Complying with the FDA is important, not only to make sure your products are legal to sell but also to make sure they will be safe for your valued customers. Let's consider some of the legal aspects here as these are important to successful bath bomb business.

COSMETICS VERSUS DRUGS AND THE FDA

When it comes to selling any type of personal care product or cosmetic you need to completely understand the rules about making claims for your product. The FDA or Food and Drug Administration created rules and regulations to protect consumers. You need to make sure your bath bombs don't make any claims that can confuse them with a drug. The FDA both defines and regulated cosmetics, drugs and soap in different ways. It can be a little confusing with these definitions to determine what is appropriate for each.

According to the FDA on their website a cosmetic is defined at the following:

"Articles intended to be rubbed, poured, sprinkled, or sprayed on, introduced into, or otherwise applied to the human body... for cleansing, beautifying, promoting attractiveness, or altering the appearance"

Based on this definition the FDA considers the following to be cosmetics:

- Moisturizers
- Perfumes
- Lipsticks
- Fingernail Polish

- Eye and Facial Makeup
- Cleansing Shampoos
- Permanent Waves
- Hair Dyes
- Deodorants

On the other hand, the FDA defines drugs as the following:

"Articles intended for use in the diagnosis, cure, mitigation, treatment, or prevention of disease"

And

"Articles (other than food) intended to affect the structure or any function of the body of man or other animals"

To simplify: a cosmetic is something used to beautify or alter appearance while a drug is used to diagnose, prevent or treat a disease or if it is intended to affect the body.

Where things get difficult is when a product can considered both a cosmetic and drug if it has two intended purposes. An example would be dandruff shampoo since it cleanses the hair as a cosmetic, but treat dandruff as a drug. If a product fits both categories then it needs to meet both requirements in order to comply with the law. Thankfully you probably won't have to worry about this when making bath bombs.

However, soap is its own category as well. There are two things the FDA uses to classify soap:

- The bulk non-volatile matter is an alkali salt of fatty acids and the detergent properties come from the alkali-fatty acid compounds and
- The product is sold, labeled and represented as nothing more than soap

When a product meets the definition of soap then it is regulated by the Consumer Product Safety Commission and not the FDA. If you claim a bath bomb does anything to alter appearance then it will be considered a cosmetic and regulated by the FDA. For example, if you claim a bath bomb can moisturize the skin.

Only drugs are required to be approved by the FDA, cosmetics and soaps don't need approval. In general, you want to avoid terms such as treat, cure and heal when labeling and/or describing your products. Some acceptable terms you can use include the following:

- Moisturizing
- Conditioning
- Calming
- Skin Friendly
- Deodorizing
- Cleansing
- Beautifying
- Hydrating

Now that we know more about the classification of cosmetic products, let's look at what you need to legally sell bath bombs.

SELLING LEGAL AND COMPLIANT PRODUCTS

- Start by obtaining a Cosmetic Product Safety Report or CPSR.
- Establish a Good Manufacturing Practice.
- Keep a Product Information File, a record of your products and each latest batch in case the public or authorities request it.
- Have a unique batch code for each product batch and keep a log with ingredients used.
- Properly label your products so people know what is in each bath bomb and how to contact you if needed.
- When in doubt, get written guidance from someone at the FDA, or from a lawyer specializing in FDA-related businesses and processes

*Important Note: This book is <u>not</u> intended to be an authoritative resource on the laws surrounding bath bombs, FDA regulations, or tax or accounting advice. I am not a lawyer or a tax professional. Do your own research and consult experts if needed. FDA and tax regulations change, and every business is unique with its own considerations.

This brings us to the third step in the process.

NAME AND PACKAGE YOUR PRODUCTS

The first interaction a customer is going to have with your bath bombs is often the packaging. Therefore, the package needs to reflect the goals of your brand while also being visually attractive to catch the customer's attention. You also need to make sure that all of your ingredients are listed properly and legally. You should also name each bath bomb batch in your inventory, preferably something that matches its scent and/or experience.

Refer to the FDA guidelines for cosmetics and aromatherapy for ensuring your label is compliant with whatever regulations you might need to comply with.

PRICE YOUR PRODUCT

If you're like me, the easy part of starting a home business is the creation of the inventory. It is fun to choose the right ingredients to bring together in a beautiful scent with a unique design. However, once you've created a great bath bomb it is time to sell your product. This is when the challenging and less fun aspect of your business start to take over and become a tedious process.

The first step in the process of selling your bath bombs is to determine how much you want to charge for your bath bombs. This may seem like a simple process of setting a price, but there is actually a lot more that goes into it and it can even be a bit confusing. When it comes to pricing bath bombs, it isn't a simple black and white process. There are a number of factors that go into determining the price of your bath bombs and the final price can be different from that of other business owners.

You need to consider distribution model, fixed costs, raw materials and labor among other things.

Before we get started on discussing the details of setting a price, the examples that I'm going to give you are just a simple number there to help give you a start in determining your pricing. In reality, you may have small costs and other things to consider that are unique to you and your business that other business owners wouldn't need to consider. It is also important to keep in mind that the numbers in your actual experience can be much higher or lower than the examples here. Simply adjust the numbers in these examples to meet your specific needs.

INDIRECT OR FIXED OVERHEAD COSTS

The first thing you want to consider is the indirect or fixed overhead costs which are often basic for small businesses of any kind. This means things like heating, electric bills, phone bills and similar. Overhead costs are often referred to as indirect or fixed costs because they stay the same. As with many similar business owners you are likely going to be working out of your own home. True overhead costs after you get past the startup phase will result in your business paying you rent.

For this example, let's say you can't make or store bath bombs in your home, so you are going to rent outside space to do it. Let's assume that renting a room to make and store your bath bombs is $200. The next you will need to add is your fixed costs such as phone/internet, heating, electric, water, sewer and garbage. Some of these costs will occur on a monthly basis, but it can also include costs that vary from month to month such as marketing materials, design work and website maintenance. This means indirect costs can vary greatly depending on the month. In the table below, I've inserted random numbers showing an average month for a small business owner. Remember that your actual costs may vary and you may have additional costs that aren't listed on this table. For example, don't forget to factor in things such as bath bomb molds.

Lastly, you don't want to forget insurance. This is essential for anyone starting a new business. Typically insurance will be about $20-$40 a month.

Rent	$200
Phone	$50
Water/Sewer	$20
Electricity	$50
Insurance	$40
Extras	$60
Total	$420

Direct Material Costs

Once you've figured out how much your indirect business costs will be for the month you need to next figure out your labor and material costs. These are often called direct costs. The actual cost of each batch of bath bombs can vary since each is likely to have slightly different ingredients.

Once you know how much of ingredients you need to produce a batch of bath bombs, you can start to calculate how much each batch will cost you. Again, this price is going to vary based on the size of ingredients you purchase. If you buy your ingredients in bulk then the cost per pound/ounce is less. This decision is up to you since buying in bulk can be cost effective in the long run, but will cost you more upfront. The main thing to consider is how many batches of soap you are able to make and sell.

However, it is also important to consider the fact that many of the oils used for fragrance do have a shelf life. Depending on how much oil you plan on using and how many batches of bath bombs you plan to make with a bath of oil you may finding buying oils in bulk to be a good idea. You may also find that how much you buy is determined by the amount of storage space you have. Yet another thing to keep in mind is the cost of shipping materials to your house.

Cost of Labor

Labor is another thing to consider when setting your prices. This is when you need to ask how much you want to pay yourself. Consider the fact that a decent wage is $15 per hour. Next, consider how long it takes you to prepare the raw materials for your bath bombs as well as the time to make the bath bombs and clean up after you're finished. Let's simplify and say it takes you a total of an hour per batch of bath bombs and that in each batch you are able to make 20 bath bombs. This means the labor cost per bath bomb would be 0.75 cents. However, this is just the cost of making the bath bombs. You'll also need to consider paying yourself for other aspects of running your business such as packaging, making sales calls and replying to customers.

Software and Fees

You might choose to use software to help run your business. Such software nowadays usually charges based on a subscription, so you will pay a little each month for something where you have access to cloud-based software. It can really help simplify how you do things, but know that these costs can add up quickly, so choose your software and subscriptions carefully.

One example is Quickbooks, which is often used to provide an accounting of your transactions in a way that makes tax time easier. Another might be a website hosting service if you want to have a website, or even something like Shopify if you plan to take transactions over the internet and ship products to customers. Don't forget about the fees on things like a PO Box (if you choose to use one) or your bank for a separate checking account.

Now total up the direct costs of your materials along with your labor cost per bath bomb and the indirect costs for the month. Divide this by the number of bath bombs you plan to produce and you'll get a cost per bath bomb.

HOW TO PRICE YOUR BATH BOMBS

Now that you have a price for the cost per bath bomb you need to know how much to charge in order to break even, but you still need to decide how much you want to charge in order to make a decent profit. So how do you determine what is the final price for your bath bombs? The price you choose will ultimately be up to you. There are a few different pricing strategies you can choose to use:

- Multiplier - With this strategy you multiply your costs by a specific value in order to get the final price you should charge for your bath bombs.
- Percentage - With this strategy you multiply your costs by a percentage in order to get the final price you should charge for your bath bombs.
- Fixed Amount - With this strategy you add a fixed amount to each bath bomb to get your final price you should charge for your bath bombs.

This will help you set a price for your bath bombs. However, there are also four specific pricing strategies to consider that can help you increase your profit margin.

As you can tell, a lot goes into a bath bomb business for something that is so simple to make. You need to do research, choose and purchase supplies, make the product and then sell it in order to make a profit. Before you start selling your bath bombs you want to make sure they are priced correctly, but you also want to make sure you are able to get the most out of your profit margin. There are four strategies you can use when pricing to help maximize your profit margin.

The first is known as penetration pricing. When you start a bath bomb business the biggest hurdle you are going to face is overcoming the stiff competition. One way to get customers to try your product over the competition is to price your bath bombs relatively low in order to penetrate into the existing market.

An example of this is the "introductory offer" you sometimes see on new products. While this strategy may not generate a huge revenue right away because of a low profit margin, it will have benefits in the long run. You will be using this trial to introduce a large base of people to your product so you get long term benefits from repeat customers.

The second is a fixed amount pricing. This is the simple act of determining a fixed price and adding it on top of the cost you want to sell your bath bombs for. This is the most popular option with most small business owners since it allows them to know the specific amount of gross profit margin that an individual sale will generate. However, if you choose this option you will have a difficult time showing a competitive price within the bath bomb market.

Another option is psychological pricing. This is when you assign a specific price point so that buyers think they are getting a deal on a product. This is based on theories that a psychological impact is placed on purchasing behavior with specific amounts. This option typically works with the buyer who wants value for their money. An example is when a buyer thinks paying $10.00 is too much, but $9.99 is cheaper and a better deal.

Lastly, there is the option of bundle pricing. With this strategy you are basically pairing two or more of your bath bombs and selling them at a price that is a little lower than if they were sold individually. This is often a preferred way to get rid of slower selling inventory. It allows your customers to feel you are giving them something for free while giving you a chance to get rid of inventory for a lower cost instead of throwing them away when they don't sell. You can also use this method to introduce new products and increase their interest among customers.

Using these methods to price your bath bombs as well as pricing to increase sales can help you make a profit from your bath bomb business. Study the industry and determine a method that works best for you, your product and your customer base.

Is There a Middleman?

If you plan to sell through an intermediary or a platform, or another business, factor that in to your pricing too.

Let's say you are selling through salons, and each bath bomb is going for $5 retail, to the customer. The salon will want to sell it for $5, which means you don't get that much. You might only get $4, $3, or in some cases $2.50, because the salon wants to make a profit for carrying your product too.

Distributors and large retailers like Target or Walmart are notorious for squeezing as much profit as possible out of suppliers, so be sure that you are factoring in all costs when selling to them. If you are lucky enough to get into Walmart with that $5 bath bomb, there is a good chance they will want to get it for $2.50 so they can make a profit on it too. You then need to ask yourself if you are able to be profitable selling all of your bath bombs for $2.50.

Now you can see why selling direct -- either at fairs and markets, or from your own website -- is so appealing. You get to keep that entire $5 for each bath bomb.

CHOOSING THE RIGHT WAY TO SELL

In order to have a successful bath bomb business you are going to need an appropriate sales channel. There are many stories of products in all industries that were incredible and groundbreaking, but without a viable way to sell them, they died in obscurity. Your business will not be like that, because you will figure out a great sales and marketing angle.

As with many businesses, a good place to start is to have a relatively passive sales process, and rely on establishing platforms to sell your bath bombs. A logical choice is having your own website and selling at online marketplaces such as Etsy. Etsy may well be a better choice for newbies, since it is a platform that already has an audience.

Having your own website is great, but you will also need to get involved in marketing and search engine optimization (SEO) in order to get people to actually visit your site. That will take some time, but if you can gradually do it, it will pay off because your profit on those sales will be greater since you are not paying a middleman like Etsy.

You should also think about some local stores in your area that would be a good places to stock your bath bombs. As we noted with the teenage bath bomb entrepreneurs in our opening chapter, they started out selling to salons in their neighborhood, after getting good market validation from local craft fairs and markets. Boutiques, massage studios, or anywhere that focuses on wellness and therapy can be a great place to start.

Then there are also local events in your area that can offer you a chance to showcase your goods and sell items. Craft fairs are great, because they are often local and not terribly expensive to exhibit at. Art fairs are great too, as long as the people there are the type who may also be looking for aromatherapy products. Don't rule out farmers markets and flea markets, which can be a great way to get an idea of who your target audience and market is. These sales channels work so well because you, as the maker, will be able to interact directly with your potential customers. That feedback directly from them is extremely valuable!

The sales channels you establish serve as the main support structure for your bath bomb business. Choose your ways to sell bath bombs carefully and try out new options to help you find what sales channel is going to be most successful for your business. We'll discuss a little more about marketing shortly.

The last step to take is to get your bath bombs out onto the market where people can purchase them directly from you, especially after you have proven the success of the product with customers. This is when you have your website in place and your physical inventory ready so you can start selling your bath bombs. This is also when you are going to start advertising online and offline to get the word out about your products. Even with the best of products, your bath bomb business won't go anywhere without successful marketing. While some companies want to ultimately sell through a retailer like Walmart or Target, 99% of small businesses will make their best profit margins from ultimately selling directly to customers.

ɔ YOUR BATH BOMB BUSINESS

ırt your bath bomb business, the first thing you

ɛrstand is seasonality and trends. This will help you

prepare ɪ̣ ɔropriate strategies for your business.

Seasons and Trends

The first thing you need to know is just what business seasonality is and how it affects your bath bomb business. Business seasonality is a term that refers to specific seasons or events that affect a business in a way that they start to lose revenue. This shouldn't scare you away from starting your bath bomb business since it can affect all types of businesses, but it can also be fought against.

As with anything, the key to success is preparation. So how can you prepare your business of seasonality? A bath bomb business relies mostly on word of mouth advertising or on your presence at local events. However, perhaps the most important part of overcoming seasonality has to do with social media marketing. This goes beyond simply selling soaps online. It also means learning as much as you can to help increase your sales at various online platforms. Consider the following three ways to improve your social media marketing.

The first thing you need to do is know your customer base. A key part of marketing bath bombs or any other type of product is to know your target audience. I'm talking about more than simply knowing who is going to want to buy your products, but rather really taking the time to get to know and understand your target audience.

In order to know both what to sell and how to sell it, you need to know what matters most to your target audience. Why are people buying your bath bombs? Which bath bomb is the most asked for and most popular? Which scent combinations are getting the most attention from customers? What makes people go online to buy your bath bombs rather than just going to the store for whatever is available? What sells best at craft fairs and other local events? Is there a specific color or texture that seems to do better? All of these can help you get to know your target audience better.

Once you've answered these questions among others then you'll have a good idea of social marketing ideas that will draw in your target audience and turn into sales even during season downturns.

The second thing you need to do is watch for trends constantly. Just as you need to get to know your target audience, you need to keep an eye on the competition and the market. Watch all the popular social media platforms such as Twitter, Pinterest and Instagram to see what people are attracted to. If there's something that's generating a lot of interest you want to get in on it.

When I say constant, I mean you need to be looking at the current trends daily. Trends in the bath bomb business and the beauty industry in general tend to change on a daily basis and you need to keep up with current trends if you want your business to stay relevant.

Lastly, make sure you stay diverse. When you stay on the lookout for trends, also keep an eye on what customers like. See if you have a slight variant that meets the customers' needs and try to diversify your offerings in order to reach a wider customer base. Take the time to learn more about the bath bomb craft and other related crafts as well. This means that when the season hits a downturn and you aren't making high sales in bath bombs then you can have a backup plan to keep your sales up and your business going.

Doing these three things will help you prepare for the inevitable down periods of business seasonality. However, what do you do when the seasons are trending up and you need to market your company and make sales? Let's look at how you can market your business both online and offline.

SELLING BATH BOMBS ONLINE

One of the more popular ways to start selling bath bombs is online through your own website or by social platforms. Two of the most popular marketplaces for selling bath bombs are Amazon and Etsy, but you can open your own online business through a number of ecommerce tools. No matter what option you choose you will want to use a number of digital marketing channels to help steer traffic to your website or online products.

The following are some good ways to steer traffic to your online products:

Instagram is a great way to build a following and provide demonstrations of your newest bath bombs. The beautiful visuals of bath bombs in the tub will help to engage your target audience.

Another option is Facebook Live. Social media such as this allows your target audience and potential customers to engage with you and gain trust and loyalty in your brand. It allows you to engage with people on a completely different level then you ever were able to in the past.

Pinterest is an option more and more home based businesses are turning to for marketing. It allows you to place visuals of your product so new customers can locate you through a visual platform.

Snapchat has a base of over 200 million users and is popular with the millennial crowd. This is a major demographic for businesses to both understand and influence. This can translate into billons of buying power at the fingertips of your business.

Don't forget about Amazon. Amazon is a massive marketplace, and every day there are probably thousands of people who are searching it for bath bombs. If you work with Amazon, the easiest way is to do Fulfillment by Amazon (FBA) where you ship a supply of bath bombs to them, and from there they basically take care of the selling and distribution for you.

They will take a larger cut of the profits than if you were to sell them directly, but the increased volume might well make up for it. Amazon is a platform like no other. If you go this route, be sure to read Amazon's terms and conditions carefully. It is important that you abide by them.

From your own website you can consider doing contests and giveaways to get the attention of your target audience. Both of these can be a powerful way for you to grow your business.

Another way to help your online business is through email marketing. This allows you to quickly and easily communicate things such as deals, promos and news to your target audiences with minimal effort and cost.

These are just a few sales channels you can use when selling your bath bombs online, but there is plenty of other options out there. You need to try several and determine which the best at helping boost your business are. Let's see how you can focus your attention once you know a good marketing platform for your business by using Instagram as an example.

10 Tips for Marketing on Instagram

Instagram is an easy way to increase popularity in your bath bomb business. Posting pictures online is a way for many people to get fame through social media these days. Everyday people are gaining millions of followers and becoming famous just by posting pictures. So there's no reason why your business can't do the same thing. As we have already seen there are plenty of social media platforms that you can use to promote your business, but when you find one that works you want to focus on it and use it to your full advantage. Let's show how you can do this by using the example of Instagram. You might be interested to know that as of 2017, 15 million businesses were registered on Instagram so it must be working. Here are ten ways you can increase your business marketing on Instagram.

The first thing you need to focus on is your pictures. A photo or picture needs to be worthy of posting on the platform. You can take advantage of this by focusing on the aesthetics of your business, which shouldn't be too hard for a bath bomb business. Often times people place more emphasis on how something looks rather than how it performs.

Since you are going to be trying to sell your bath bombs on Instagram, this means you can't simply grab any phone or camera and take pictures of your products to start uploading. Rather you need to take the time to consider editing your photos before uploading to the website. Again, keep in mind it is all about the aesthetics.

If you aren't an expert in photo editing, don't worry. There are plenty of easy to use photo editors on the internet. Photoshop is no longer something relegated to professionals only, now there are plenty of user friendly platforms that allow anyone to professionally edit photos. Plus there are plenty of free programs so you don't have to increase your marketing budget exponentially just to get good looking photos.

Even if photo editing software doesn't work for you, there are still solutions. Instagram offers built-in filters that you can use to do some basic touch ups on your photos before posting.

Second, make sure you post a variety of things. Rather than simply posting pictures of your products and hoping people will buy them, you need to keep things fresh and interesting. Think of all the different ways you can post photos of your products. Photograph your products with a pleasing background that enhances the scent or color of your bath bombs.

Another option is to post photos during your creation process. People enjoy seeing how a product is made and makes the products more personal for people so they are more likely to make a purchase. Plus seeing the time and effort that goes into making your products will make people feel like they are getting a better value for your bath bombs so it can be used as a part of your pricing strategy as well.

You can even invite customers to post images of the products being used in their own homes. This way people can get a real world example of your products and see that others are enjoying what you have to offer.

You want to also keep things diverse by alternating between business and fun posts. There is no limit to the memes or quotes you can post, but just make sure you keep it relevant to your products as well as the image you want your business and brand to project. You can even upload more than one photo at once to show how your bath bombs are made. Keep a record of which posts get the most attention so you can understand your target audience and what they like to see. This way you can cater your Instagram posts to your customers and help boost your sales.

The third key point is to use the hashtag, but don't overdo it. Too much of a good thing can be a bad thing. When trying to sell products or advertise a business on Instagram you want to keep your hashtags toned down and only use those that are relevant to your products and businesses. While each post can have up to 30 hashtags, this doesn't mean you have to use them all. It is best to have two to three consistent hashtags that you use for each post and then add a few extra for your specific product or promotion you are running.

Another thing is to consider putting your hashtags in a separate comment rather than in the caption. Putting a lot of hashtags in the caption can be confusing and cluttering. Either way works, but just determine what looks best for your business and works best at drawing in your target audience.

The fourth thing is to make sure you have an effective business bio. Let's say you post a series of photos on how you make your bath bombs and they are a hit with your target audience. Now you have interested people who want to know more. The next thing these people are going to do is visit your profile.

The Instagram business profile can be tricky. You only have 150 characters to work with. This means you have a limited amount of ways to impress your potential customers. This means you need to clearly define what your business is about, what you are and encourage people to keep engaging with your business. You should include a link to your website in the bio since people can't click on a link in the captions.

Potential customers can then go to your website if they want to know more about your company and the products you offer. Instagram also offers other Call-To-Action options, so you'll want to pick the right ones for your business and utilize them appropriately.

The fifth thing is to have a good posting plan or schedule in place. Social media is addictive to people today, but even more so for the business owner. You need to check into social media and update your posts on a daily basis if you plan to get anywhere with your customer base. However, this doesn't mean you want to constantly flood Instagram with photos and posts about your business. There needs to be a fine line between keeping your business at the forefront of peoples' minds and becoming the annoying business that people walk away from. You want to time your posts for when Instagram traffic is the highest. Based on marketing research the best times for Instagram are the following:

- Monday: 7 and 10 pm
- Tuesday: 3 am and 10 pm
- Wednesday: 5 pm
- Thursday: 7 am and 11 pm

- Friday: 1 am and 8 pm
- Saturday: 12 am and 2 am
- Sunday: 5 pm

The sixth thing you want to consider is videos. Instagram doesn't have to be limited to photos only. You can upload a video and let people see you creating a beautiful bath bomb. There are two ways to use Instagram's video services.

First you can take and stream a live video. This can be a great way to give customers a behind the scenes look at your business and how your products are made. People can leave comments or questions and you can answer them live. After the stream is done, it will stay on Instagram Stories for 24 hours.

If this doesn't seem like an option for you, the second choice is to upload video from your camera or phone. You also have the option of filming a video directly through Instagram. Consider posting a tutorial or a behind the scenes clip, something engaging and unique.

While you're not guaranteed success with these options, it is another tool. It doesn't hurt to try it at least once and see what happens. The worst that can happen is it won't be effective and you don't use it again. The main thing is to experiment with or research times that are best for you and your business as well as your target audience. Schedule your posts accordingly and you'll get the best results.

For the seventh thing I'm going to go back to something I've mentioned a few times already, behind the scenes. When you post a video or image of your business behind the scenes it gives people are more personal touch. If you just use Instagram to sell your bath bombs people are going to see you as a business and they won't want any deeper of a connection. When you humanize yourself you are creating an emotional attachment with your potential customers that in turn makes you more relatable and this helps to boost your sales.

It also encourages people to follow you and interact with you, this can be like an internet version of word of mouth. Just make sure you make time to respond to comments so your audience knows they are being heard and that you care about what they are saying. It can also be a valuable tool in finding out what your target audience wants so you can prepare bath bombs that are going to sell rather than simply take up your inventory.

We briefly touched on number eight before, but let's look a little closer at doing contests and giveaways. Nothing keeps people interested more than giving away free stuff. Contests allow you to engage with your target audience and provides you with an excellent way to promote your business. The best thing about contests is it can lead to you getting more followers on Instagram and more potential customers.

On Instagram one of the most popular forms of contest is obviously the Photo Contest. Ask your target audience to post specific photos with a certain contest hashtag. This hashtag will get you a lot of additional exposure. Another type of contest you can choose to do is the Likes Contest or Like to Win Contest. This is a fast and simple option. Lastly, the Tag-A-Friend Contest is always popular because it allows you to spread your business out to family and friends of loyal customers, similar to a word of mouth campaign offline.

Another option is to do a weekly giveaway. This is a great option since it also allows your Instagram page to get weekly activity. The activity doesn't have to be huge, but it will be enough to prevent your bath bomb business from disappearing amongst the competition. Also remember to regram or repost things your followers post that feature your business or product. People enjoy when they are featured or recognized.

The second to the last tip is to make sure you follow back. This works very similar to networking. The more you and your business branches out the more you will see benefits. Focus on your followers by sending shout outs and they may return the favor. This is free advertising for your business. You can do this anytime of the week.

Shout outs don't just have to be for your followers, you can also do it for other businesses in the same field as yours. This may seem odd at first, but it is a great way to create partnerships where both can have mutual benefits. Consider partnering with someone in the beauty field that sells soaps or other similar businesses. This gives you more exposure and widens your target audience while doing the same for your partner.

Lastly, make sure you connect to Facebook. No everyone who has Instagram has Facebook so why would you want to connect on Facebook? Because the reverse is also true, not everyone who has Facebook also has Instagram. In fact, your followers may notice you have both Facebook and Instagram accounts so they may start following you on other social media platforms. You can also have contests and deals exclusively for Instagram followers and then share this news on your Facebook feed so you get new followers on your Instagram feed.

Whenever you post a video or photo on Instagram, you are given the option of sharing it on Facebook and other social media platforms so why not do it. Share everywhere and you're going to be getting the word out to quite a few people. People don't think twice about sharing posts they enjoy on social media so there's no reason you shouldn't share your posts with other social media platforms.

There are the ten ways you can increase your marketing strategy for Instagram. You can apply many of these strategies to other social media platforms as well. The main thing is to find a social media platform that works well for your business and capitalize on it by doing all you can to attract your target audience. However, you can't rely totally on online marketing and sales. So now let's take a look at how you can sell your bath bombs offline and make a profit.

SELLING BATH BOMBS OFFLINE

New and small business owners don't need to limit themselves to online selling only, many at home businesses do well with offline selling as well. Let's take a look at some ways you can sell offline and how you can increase your profit margin while selling offline.

First, let us consider just why you want to consider selling offline in a world that is dominated by online. When you sell in person you are access a completely new target audience and you will be able to get live and instant feedback about your products. The best opportunities for small businesses is to use market booths at craft fairs and pop-up shops to get a temporary retail location without the cost of paying for a high storefront rent or a long lease. Plus it gives you the chance to sell alongside other talented people who can give you inspiration for future products. Some other reasons to consider selling offline and in person include the following:

Selling offline is like have a live product testing ground. You can get direct feedback and questions from potential customers. Hearing concerns allows you to gain invaluable insight into how you can improve your products and address common concerns that may be preventing people from purchasing your products.

Depending on the offline areas where you sell you can also gain access to potential wholesale clients. Markets and fairs are often attended by a range of retailers who are looking for new and innovative products for their stores. This is a great chance for a small business owner to connect with a wholesale outlet and a big increase in their sales.

Offline can also be an excellent way to build your online following. You can turn the connections you meet at fairs, markets and festivals into email subscribers or social media followers.

Lastly, offline events are a great way to meet with fellow business owners, makers and entrepreneurs. This can help you build a strong network that will offer you added benefits and broaden the range of your business.

While selling offline may seem more intimidating then doing things online, it is actually fairly easy and very rewarding. There are plenty point-of-sale systems that make it easy for you to sell at a variety of locations such as flea markets, craft fairs and farmers' markets. If you want to sell your products offline then consider the following nine tips to help you increase your profits when selling offline.

Today, the attraction of craft fairs and farmers' markets have risen to include a range of businesses that meet a variety of needs. These small fairs provide a very inviting atmosphere encourages customers to interact with vendors in a comfortable and convenient environment. To maximize your benefits and profits from these offline selling endeavors there are nine things you need to do.

Tips for Selling Offline

First, you need to be personable and tell your story. When you go to a craft fair or farmers' market you get an interaction with potential customers that you don't get when selling online. Being at these events adds a personal touch that allows you to share your story and tell people why you are doing what you're doing. Talk to people about why you decided to start making and selling bath bombs. Telling people about the background of your products and business is a great conversation starter and can help you show people how your products are going to benefit them.

Second, selling offline has something that selling online doesn't have: packaging. Admit it, you've probably bought an item at some point simply because of how the packaging looked. A product such as a bath bomb not only needs to look appealing, but it also needs to have attractive packaging. The packaging needs to complement and reflect your brand as well as the feel of your product.

It is also important to have a good name for your products and collections. There is a few things you need to consider when naming your products. The name needs to be both relevant to the product and also something that makes it easier for the customer to recall. The best way to create a name that customers recall is to focus on the benefits, using a witty play on words or creating a personality that resonates with the customer.

We talked about business seasonality earlier and the fourth thing to do is to use that seasonality. Create collections on top of your current inventory by offering them during a specific time that is aligned with a seasonal theme. This way you are not only targeting current buyer's needs, but you're also creating a new potential customer pool from the family and friends that are likely to receive them as gifts. This is a great way to increase your brands awareness and word of mouth marketing.

When selling products offline it is important that you work to turn buyers into followers. While offline selling is important and has its benefits, there is nothing more valuable than a social media presence. You need to create a community of online followers who are updated to your new offerings and where they can purchase your product. You are able to create this online community through offline selling by encouraging people to like or follow your page to get more ideas about bath bombs such as how to make them, recipes and samples that they can take home for free.

When selling offline you may choose to increase your sales through product bundling. This is one of the oldest marketing tricks in the book. You create promotional bundles by putting together a few of your products. This can be a great way to increase awareness about what your brand has to offer and encourages people to try new products or to clear out inventory of items that aren't as often purchased as your bestsellers.

Especially at craft fairs and farmers' markets you want to have an interactive booth setup. The booth needs to be visually appealing and it needs to stand out from the rest of the booths. This will attract and invite more people to approach your booth and gives you more opportunities to talk about your business and products. Make sure you have samples from your collection available for people to touch, smell or even try in order to offer a more personal and memorable experience.

The second to the last tip may not work as well for a bath bomb business, but you never know. You may want to consider a product for a cause. Integrate your business with a social responsibility. Do this by contacting a charity that can benefit from your product or has a similar interest to your business. Let customers know about your businesses charitable involvement so they know they are not only purchasing a good product, but they are also support people or a good cause.

Lastly, when selling offline make sure you have compelling offers. Research offers that are attractive to potential customers in your area and then implement them when you go to events in the area. Promotions can encourage people to buy even if they aren't looking for your particular product in the first place.

Getting your product in the hands of potential customers is the best way to boost a loyal following by using the above nine strategies. Just remember to assess your business performance after each even so you can learn from your experience and further your business.

THE ALL-IMPORTANT LABEL

When selling offline, or online for that matter, you will find that it is incredibly important to do a great job with your bath bomb label. Think about it -- if you buy a bath bomb at a craft fair, come home, and use it and love it, the only thing allowing you to buy more is to find the label and order additional units. Make sure your label makes it easy for people to do that.

First, be sure to have a label that will stick with people. Put a splash of color on it, but don't make it too busy. You might want to use an image, or you might simpy want to use your company's name with a catchy font. Remember that the label size will likely be small, so the more words you try to jam on it, the less anyone will actually read it.

Second, always put information on your label about where people can get more bath bombs! Perhaps you want them to go to your website. If so, print it on the label! Or maybe you want to have them go to Amazon to get more. Say that. People want to know it is easy to restock.

Finally, if there is something unique about your bath bombs, reinforce it on the label. Maybe your bath bombs are all natural. Say it. Or perhaps your bath bombs are made from real lavender, or something else. Maybe yours are made locally. Perhaps proceeds form your bath bombs go to charity. Those notes, if it doesn't require too much space, can make a big impact.

CONCLUSION

So there you have it. Everything you needed to know about the bath bomb trend and business environment. What you need to know to make bath bombs and start your very own from home business. In closing I would like to give you five helpful tips to keep in mind when starting your business and while running it for years to come.

First, focus on what you do best and leave the rest to others. The primary disadvantage of a work from home business is that production takes up a lot of your time and you don't have much left for actually running your business. Without sacrificing the art of making handmade products, what potential tasks can you give to someone else? Perhaps you can be responsible for the fine details while leaving other parts of the prep work to others. If you prefer to focus solely on the making of your bath bombs then perhaps you can hire a freelance individual to help with fulfillment, shipping and customer service. Or perhaps there are ways you can automate your business so you can focus more on the tasks you are good at.

Second, never undervalue your work. As you seen earlier, pricing handmade goods can be challenging. You not only need to consider your time in making the bath bombs, but you also need to place a value on your products' uniqueness and artistry.

Follow the general guidelines for pricing, but make sure you factor in your labor and don't undervalue your talent.

Third, make sure you educate your target audience and potential customers. Handmade items need to be priced higher than mass produced items. However, what makes a person want to pay more for a handmade item than a mass produced item is the uniqueness, ethical production and craftsmanship. You need to make people aware of this through education. Include it in your site copy as well as your product pages and FAQs. Make sure your customers know why they are paying more and why buying homemade is worth their extra money.

Fourth, keep it personal and tell your story. Tell people about your homemade process and your personal journey to creating your business. Do this in marketing through videos and blogs. With a strong and consistent voice on social media you will be able to represent yourself and your brand. Customers will often buy from smaller businesses because they are buying into the lifestyle that went into making the brand or because they want to buy a piece of the person making the product. Be sure to highlight what makes you stand out from the competition and focus on the things that larger businesses can't such as the personal and one of a kind experience.

Lastly, consider expanding your business with custom and made-to-order services. When you make handmade products you have something that most other companies can't offer. You can tailor products to your customer's needs. When you offer custom and made-to-order services you can greatly increase your production as people will come to you for that unique and special item they can't get anywhere else.

Now you are well and truly ready to go out there and start putting together your inventory because you're going to have a booming bath bomb business in no time.

****

If you enjoyed this book or found it useful, please consider leaving a review. Your review is extremely important to me personally and to future readers!

Printed by Amazon Italia Logistica S.r.l.
Torrazza Piemonte (TO), Italy

17401107R00039